Kids Top 10 Pet Birds

Wendy Mead

Enslow Elementary

an imprint of

Enslow Publishers, Inc.

40 Industrial Road
Box 398
Berkeley Heights, NJ 07922
USA

http://www.enslow.com

AMERICAN HUMANE ASSOCIATION
EST. 1877

American Humane Association is the country's first national humane organization and the only one dedicated to protecting both children and animals. Since 1877, American Humane Association has been at the forefront of virtually every major advance in protecting our most vulnerable from cruelty, abuse and neglect. Today we're also leading the way in understanding the human-animal bond and its role in therapy, medicine and society. American Humane Association reaches millions of people every day through groundbreaking research, education, training and services that span a wide network of organizations, agencies and businesses. You can help make a difference, too. Visit American Humane Association at www.americanhumane.org today.

To Our Readers: We have done our best to make sure all Internet addresses in this book were active and appropriate when we went to press. However, the author and the publisher have no control over and assume no liability for the material available on those Internet sites or on other Web sites they may link to. Any comments or suggestions can be sent by e-mail to comments@enslow.com or to the address on the back cover.

Every effort has been made to locate all copyright holders of material used in this book. If any errors or omissions have occurred, corrections will be made in future editions of this book.

♻ Enslow Publishers, Inc., is committed to printing our books on recycled paper. The paper in every book contains 10% to 30% post-consumer waste (PCW). The cover board on the outside of each book contains 100% PCW. Our goal is to do our part to help young people and the environment too!

Enslow Elementary, an imprint of Enslow Publishers, Inc.

Enslow Elementary® is a registered trademark of Enslow Publishers, Inc.

Copyright © 2015 by Enslow Publishers, Inc.

Originally published as *Top 10 Birds for Kids* in 2009.

Library of Congress Cataloging-in-Publication Data
Mead, Wendy, author.
  [Top 10 birds for kids]
  Kids top 10 pet birds / Wendy Mead.
     pages cm. — (American Humane Association Top 10 pets for kids)
  "Originally published as Top 10 Birds for Kids in 2009."
  Summary: "Discusses the best ten birds for kids to keep as pets and includes each species' appearance, general behavior, and special needs."— Provided by publisher.
  Audience: K to grade 3.
  Includes bibliographical references and index.
  ISBN 978-0-7660-6625-0
  1. Cage birds—Juvenile literature. 2. Pets—Juvenile literature. I. Title. II. Title: Kids top ten pet birds.
  SF461.35.M43 2015
  636.6'8—dc23
                                    2014026094

Future Editions:
Paperback ISBN: 978-0-7660-6626-7
EPUB ISBN: 978-0-7660-6627-4
Single-User PDF ISBN: 978-0-7660-6628-1
Multi-User PDF ISBN: 978-0-7660-6629-8

Printed in the United States of America
102014 Bang Printing, Brainerd, Minn.
10 9 8 7 6 5 4 3 2 1

Interior Photo Credits: iStockphoto.com: Eric Isselée, p. 23 (budgie); EuToch, pp. 4 (cockatiel), 27 (cockatiel); Jill Lang, pp. 20, 41 (parakeet); webphotographeer, p. 19. Shutterstock.com: Andrew Burgess, p. 47 (parakeet); Daniel Hixon, p. 30; EBFoto, p. 8; Eduardo Rivero, p. 34; Elena Blokhina, p. 6; Eric Isselée, pp. 9 (finch), 14 (canary), 24, 25 (canary); Four Oaks, p. 28; Jill Lang, p. 11; Kevin H Knuth, p. 37 (parrotlets); kimmik, p. 5; KonstantinChristian, p. 15; Lori Martin, p. 40; panbazil, p. 1 (budgies); Panu Ruangjan, p. 38; photovova, p. 42 (lovebird); Pichugin Dmitry, p. 39 (lovebirds); Theodore Scott, p. 10; Tracy Starr, p. 32; waldru, p. 44; Wang LiQiang, p. 31 (finches). © Thinkstock: Jill Lang/iStock, p. 17; leidy755/iStock, p. 35 (parakeet); Norasit Kaewsa/iStock, p. 22; odole/iStock, p. 13; Olmarmar/iStock, p. 26; panupong1982/iStock, p. 36; Robert Blanchard/iStock, p. 29 (dove).

Cover Credit: Petar Ivanov Ishmiriev/Shutterstock.com (blue and yellow budgie).

The top ten birds are approved by the American Humane Association and are listed alphabetically.

Contents

So You Want to Get a Bird?

Have you ever watched a bird fly through the air? Or listened to the different sounds and songs birds can make? Maybe you have even seen a bird perform a trick or two. Then you know just how amazing these animals can be.

Some birds are wild and should stay outside. Others can be taught to live inside with people.

Cockatiels are popular pet birds. Birds that become pets have been raised to rely on humans for their care.

Kids Top 10 Pet Birds

Most pet birds love to fly. They also enjoy playing with toys or with their owners. Some pet birds can even talk, copying the words they hear from humans.

Birds can be fun pets, but they need to be treated gently. They can be easily startled or hurt. So birds are not a good choice for a pet if you want an animal that you can chase around. Pet birds also need a lot of care. They need fresh water and food every day. Their cages, dishes, and toys need to be cleaned regularly.

Deciding whether to get a pet bird is a big decision. There are many questions

There are many kinds of pet birds that like to be handled. Some, such as budgies, even like to play with their owners.

So You Want to Get a Bird?

you and your family should consider when thinking about getting a pet bird:

1. Do you have the time for daily feedings and cage care?

2. Will you make sure that your bird gets enough exercise?

3. Will you give your bird the attention it needs?

4. Will other members of your family help care for your bird?

Birds can live long lives. Some kinds can live up to thirty years. Be sure you are ready for this before you get your new pet. Remember, you are going to be friends for many years to come.

What kind of "personality" do you want your pet to have? The Indian ringneck parakeet has a loud voice and is very active.

How to Choose a Pet Bird

There are more than ten thousand species, or types, of birds. But only some of these species make good pets, and each of them is different from one another. Some birds are loud and busy. Others are quieter and calmer. Some birds like to be handled. Others enjoy staying in their cages. What kind of pet do you want?

Some birds, such as finches, are happiest living in groups or pairs. Others enjoy living alone in their cages.

Besides how a bird acts, you need to think about its size. You should consider the size of your home. Do you want a small bird or a large bird?

You also have to decide how many birds you want. Some birds can be kept alone. But others need another bird to keep them company. For example, if you really like finches, it would be best for you to get a pair of them. Sometimes different types of birds can be kept together. Be sure to find out which ones can live together peacefully.

How to Choose a Pet Bird

Once you know what kind of bird you want, there are many places you can go to get your new pet. A bird rescue group is a great place to find birds that need homes. Pet stores also offer many birds to choose from. But be sure to check out any store before buying a bird there. Is it clean? Does it look like the birds have fresh food and water? Do they have room to move around?

Check out a pet store before you buy a bird there. Make sure the store is clean and that all the birds are treated well.

Another way to get a bird is to go to a bird breeder, a person who raises and sells birds. A breeder usually raises one type of bird and knows a lot about that bird. As with a pet store, you should first look and see how the birds are being treated.

No matter where you go to find your bird, you will want to know if the bird has been hand-fed. This means it has been cared for by humans since it was young and is used to being handled. Birds raised this way are usually tamer than those raised by their own bird parents.

When looking for a pet, check for signs that a bird is healthy. A healthy bird will move around in the cage. It will have clear eyes and nostrils. Check out its legs to see if they are clean and straight. Look at its feet and claws to make sure they are not damaged. Also look at the vent area, which is where the bird releases its waste. It should be clean.

Think about getting an adult bird instead of a young one. It might be calmer than a younger bird and might already be trained. Adult birds can be found through rescue groups and newspaper ads. Make sure to ask if

How to Choose a Pet Bird

the bird is healthy or if it seems to have any bad habits. Getting an older bird can be a great way to find a new pet friend.

Take your time when picking out a pet bird. The bird you choose will probably be with you for a long time.

Healthy birds are active and have bright, clean eyes and feathers.

Creating Your Bird's "Nest"

A good home for your bird will include the right cage, perches, dishes, and toys. Different birds need different types of cages. A canary might be comfortable in a small cage. But that same cage would not be big enough for a Quaker parakeet to stretch its wings. As a general rule, try to get the largest cage possible for your pet. There should be enough room for your bird to fly around.

Creating Your Bird's "Nest"

No matter the size of your bird, make sure there is room for water and food dishes, perches, and toys.

The cage should be strong, too. Make sure the bars are sturdy and made of metal. It is important that the distance between the bars is right for your type of bird. Usually, smaller birds need a shorter distance between the bars so they cannot squeeze out.

You will also need a cage cover. Covering the cage tells the bird that it is time to rest. You can buy paper liners or use newspaper to cover the bottom of the cage to collect droppings and discarded food.

Kids Top 10 Pet Birds

Get a few perches, or rods, for the bird to rest and play on. Use different widths to provide your bird with some choices, just like in the wild. You can also add a ladder for your bird to climb on.

You will also need dishes for food and water. Pick dishes that fit the needs of your bird. Small plastic dishes that clip onto the side of the cage will work for smaller birds. But larger birds may need stronger dishes made of metal.

Water can also be given to your bird using a water bottle that attaches to the cage. No matter what kind of dish or bottle you choose, make sure to clean them often.

Toys can help your bird enjoy its new home. Chew toys are popular with many kinds of birds. Your bird might also enjoy playing on a swing. You could even give a small bird a ping pong ball to push around its cage. Toys are usually made for different sizes of birds. So make sure to get the ones that are right for your pet.

Like humans, birds can get bored, so make sure to change the toys every week. For birds that spend time outside of their cage, you might want to get a play gym.

Creating Your Bird's "Nest"

A play gym is a stand that has perches, ladders, and other toys to entertain the bird.

Having a comfortable cage and other supplies will help your bird adjust to its new home.

Bringing Your Bird Home

Before you bring your bird home, think about where you want to put its cage. Once you pick a place for the cage, it is best to keep it there. Being moved around a lot

Many birds enjoy playing with toys. If you trade out the toys in your birds' cage from week to week, you can keep them from getting bored.

Bird Basics

1. Cage
2. Cage cover
3. Cage paper liners
4. Food dish
5. Water dish or bottle
6. Food
7. Perches
8. Toys

could be upsetting to your new pet. Because birds can be sensitive, it is important to pick just the right spot.

Birds need light and warmth. To keep them healthy, place the cage away from any drafts and not directly in front of any window. A bright corner of the living room could be a good spot for your bird.

For the first few days, try to keep the house quiet. Your new bird needs some time to get comfortable in its new home. Keep visitors away until the bird has gotten settled. Make sure to walk up to the bird slowly and talk to it softly. Be patient. It will take a little time for you and your new bird friend to get used to each other.

If you can, try to take your bird for a checkup on the same day you buy the bird. Bird owners take their pets to

Creating Your Bird's "Nest"

an avian veterinarian (vet). This is an animal doctor who works with birds. Have the vet look at your bird for any health problems.

Feeding Your Bird

Your new feathered friend needs you to make sure it gets plenty of food and water. Bird experts say to feed birds

Soon after you get your bird, bring it to the vet. Then you can be sure your pet is healthy.

Most birds eat seeds. But conures and some other kinds of birds also eat cooked meat and eggs.

a diet made of different types of food. Many of them say that birds should eat mostly pellets. Pellets are a special type of food that comes in small pieces. There are different types of pellets for nearly every type of pet bird.

Others like to give their birds some seeds, too. Check with your vet about whether pellets or seeds are right for your bird.

Creating Your Bird's "Nest"

Fruits and vegetables are good for birds, just like they are for humans. Apple slices and shredded carrots are common bird snacks. Some birds also like to have a bit of hard-boiled egg or cooked meat every once in a while.

Water is also important to keep your bird healthy. It should be as clean as possible. Change the water at least once a day.

No matter what kind of bird you have, there are some foods you should never give it. Avocados, chocolate, and fruit seeds and pits are all foods that can make your bird very sick. Also, never let your bird drink coffee or alcohol.

Budgies are quieter than many other birds.

Appearance

- Some budgies have a yellow face with blue around the nostrils and on the cheeks, a green chest, and yellow, black, and blue feathers on the wings and back.

- Other budgies are mostly yellow with small patches of white on the face. Still others are mostly blue or gray with white and/or black on the head, back, and wings.

- Length: 7 inches

Budgies are playful. They can also learn to talk but are usually pretty quiet. No wonder they are such popular pets!

Chapter 1

Budgie

Budgies are the most popular type of pet bird in the United States. Their official name is budgerigar (BUD-jer-ree-ger), but they are called "budgies" for short. These cute, small birds are a type of parakeet originally from Australia.

General Behavior

Budgies:

1. are active and playful.

2. can learn to talk.

3. like to bathe.

4. are quieter than many other birds.

5. can get fat if you overfeed them.

6. live about 7 years.

Special Needs

Budgies like to fly, so a tall, rectangular cage is a good choice for them. Make sure it is at least 18 inches long by 18 inches wide by 24 inches high. They also need to spend time out of their cage for exercise.

Canaries are cheerful and active.

The German roller (above) and the Gloster fancy (right) are just two of the many kinds of pet canaries.

Appearance

- Many canaries are mostly yellow with touches of white and sometimes brown on the face, head, chest, wings, and tail.

- There are also red canaries with white or brown on the face, head, wings, and tail.

- Length: 4 to 8 inches

Chapter 2

Canary

Canaries are originally from the Canary Islands, which are located off the northwest coast of Africa. They now can be found all over the world as pets. The German roller, border, American singer, Gloster fancy, Belgian fancy, and Norwich are all types of canaries.

General Behavior

Canaries:

1. are cheerful and active.

2. are known for their singing (males only).

3. make chirping sounds (females).

4. are quieter than many other pet birds.

5. do not like being handled.

6. live about 10 years.

Special Needs

Canaries should have a rectangular cage that is at least 18 inches long by 12 inches wide by 12 inches high. They prefer to stay in their cage, so it should be large enough for flying around.

Cockatiels are known for being cuddly and gentle.

Appearance

- Cockatiels usually have gray bodies with yellow faces and orange patches on their cheeks. They also can have white, yellow, and brown bodies.

- All cockatiels have a crest, which is a group of feathers that stick up on the top of their head, as well as a long tail.

- Length: 12 inches

Cockatiels enjoy spending time out of their cage for exercise and play.

Chapter 3

Cockatiel

Cockatiels are one of the world's most popular pet birds. They are a type of parrot and are originally from Australia.

General Behavior

Cockatiels:

1. are known for being cuddly and gentle.

2. love attention.

3. can be good at whistling.

4. can be great at copying the sounds and noises around them.

5. are not as noisy as some other parrots.

6. can develop a biting problem.

7. live about 18 years.

Special Needs

Cockatiels have long tails, so be sure to choose a cage that is at least 24 inches tall to give the bird enough room. They also like to spend time out of their cage to exercise and play with their owners. If not gently tamed, cockatiels can become biters.

Doves make a quiet cooing sound.

Diamond doves are one of the most popular pet doves. All doves are quiet and gentle birds.

Appearance

- Doves come in several colors, including white and brown.

- All doves have long, narrow beaks and many have a ring of brightly colored skin around their eyes.

- The ringneck dove gets its name from the dark half-circle markings on the back of its neck.

- Length: 7 ½ to 12 inches

Chapter 4

Dove

Doves are a smaller type of pigeon found all over the world. There are more than three hundred species of doves and pigeons. Some of the most popular kinds of pet doves include the diamond dove, Barbary or ringneck dove, and the mourning dove.

General Behavior

Doves:

1. are peaceful and gentle.
2. are quiet and make a cooing sound.
3. are best kept in pairs.
4. might build a nest if they have materials such as long, dry pine needles.
5. live 12 to 15 years.

Special Needs

Doves exercise inside their cages, so they need a lot of room to move around. They should have a cage that is at least 24 inches long by 24 inches wide by 24 inches tall.

There are many species of finches.

Finches are some of the most colorful pet birds. Popular ones are Gouldian finches (left) and zebra finches (right).

Appearance

- Finches come in many colors, including red, purple, green, orange, gray, brown, and blue.

- The zebra finch has a red beak; gray, white, and black feathers on the face, wings, and tail; and a light tan chest.

- The Gouldian finch is brightly colored, with red or orange around the eyes, a purple chest, yellow belly, and green back.

- Length: 3 to 8 inches

Chapter 5

Finch

Finches are small birds that come from Africa, Asia, and Australia. There are several species of finches. Zebra, Gouldian, and society finches are some of them. They cannot be tamed and prefer to stay in their cage.

General Behavior

Finches:

1. are active and lively.

2. are quieter than many other birds.

3. are not tame and do not like to be handled.

4. must be kept in pairs.

5. live 4 to 10 years.

Special Needs

Finches stay in their cages, so they need a home that they can exercise in. A long, rectangular cage that is at least 14 inches long by 24 inches wide by 18 inches high will be best for them.

Green-cheeked conures can learn to play games with their owner.

Green-cheeked conures are curious birds. They love to spend time exercising and playing outside their cage.

Appearance

- The green-cheeked conure has a long tail and a curved, gray beak. It usually has a brown head with green cheeks and a white ring around the eyes.

- The body is green and maroon with white and gray around the chest and a maroon tail.

- Length: 10 inches

Chapter 6

Green-Cheeked Conure

Green-cheeked conures (CON-yers) come from South America. They are usually found in parts of Argentina, Bolivia, and Brazil. The green-cheeked is just one of the many kinds of conures. Sun, dusky, red-fronted, and maroon-bellied conures are other species.

General Behavior

Green-cheeked conures:

1. are friendly, curious, and playful.

2. can learn to play games with their owner.

3. like to chew.

4. can be very noisy.

5. may nip and bite if not trained properly.

6. live about 10 years.

Special Needs

Because of their long tails and active nature, green-cheeked conures need a big cage. Look for one that is at least 24 inches long by 24 inches wide by 36 inches high. Conures are sometimes known for nipping or biting people while being handled. This can sometimes be fixed with proper training.

Indian ringneck parakeets can learn to do tricks and to talk.

Appearance

- The Indian ringneck parakeet has a reddish-orange beak and very long tail. It usually has a green head and body with some blue in the tail.

- The male has a rose and black ring around the neck, and the female has a faint, light-green ring around the neck.

- Indian ringnecks can now also be found in blue, white, and yellow.

- Length: about 16 inches

Indian ringneck parakeets play with toys, climb play gyms, and stretch their wings for exercise.

Chapter 7

Indian Ringneck Parakeet

The Indian ringneck parakeet can be found in Asia and Africa. It is just one of the ringnecked parakeets. Others include the African ringneck and Neumann's ringneck.

General Behavior

Indian ringneck parakeets:

1. love to show off and receive attention.
2. can learn to do tricks and to talk.
3. can copy the sounds around them.
4. like to chew.
5. can be very noisy at times.
6. need to be handled every day to stay tame.
7. live 20 to 25 years.

Special Needs

Large birds such as Indian ringneck parakeets need a roomy cage that is about 24 inches long by 24 inches wide by 36 inches tall. To stay fit, they need to spend about an hour out of their cage every day to exercise.

Parrotlets are the smallest type of parrot.

Appearance

- The parrottet has a large beak and short tail, and comes in several colors.

- The Pacific parrottet usually has a light green face with blue markings on the back of the head and grayish-green wings with blue or gray feathers. But they have been bred to be mostly blue with gray and to be several different shades of yellow. Other color patterns are available, too.

- Length: 4 to 6 inches

Parrotlets, such as the Pacific parrotlet (above) and the Mexican parrotlet (right), are the smallest type of parrot.

Chapter 8

Parrotlet

Parrotlets are the smallest type of parrot. They are usually less than 6 inches long, while their other parrot cousins can be between 9 and 16 inches in length. There are many types of parrotlets. The most common ones are the Pacific, the Mexican, and the green rumped. Parrotlets come from South America, Mexico, and other parts of Latin America.

General Behavior

Parrotlets:

1. are social and playful.
2. need a lot of attention.
3. like to bathe.
4. can be moody.
5. can bite.
6. usually live more than 20 years.

Special Needs

Parrotlets are busy birds that enjoy playing and moving around a lot. They need a cage that is at least 18 inches long by 18 inches wide by 18 inches tall. They also like to be let out of their cage to explore and exercise.

Lovebirds like to be kept in pairs.

Lovebirds like to chew. A supply of millet (a kind of seed) is a good thing for them to nibble on.

Appearance

- Most lovebirds have short, bright-green bodies and short tails. The face is an orangey-peach color and has a curved, light-colored beak.

- There are also lovebirds that have yellow bodies with reddish faces and ones with bluish-green bodies and yellow and white faces and chests.

- Length: 5 to 7 inches

Chapter 9

Peach-Faced Lovebird

These smart birds are just one of the many kinds of lovebirds. They are originally from Africa. Fischer's lovebirds and masked lovebirds are also popular pets.

General Behavior

Lovebirds:

1. are smart and hardy.
2. like to bathe.
3. can be loud at times.
4. need to be handled often to keep tame.
5. are best kept as a pair, as your only pets.
6. live 10 to 12 years.

Special Needs

Peach-faced lovebirds like to fly and should have a tall, rectangular cage. Look for a cage that is at least 14 inches long by 24 inches wide by 30 inches tall. They also like to get out of their cage to exercise.

Quaker parakeets are talkative and lively.

Appearance

- The Quaker parakeet has a long tail and short, curved orange beak.

- Most have green bodies and wings with gray feathers on the face and chest. Breeders have also created a mostly blue Quaker parakeet with light gray cheeks and chest. There are also some Quaker parakeets that are yellow with white in their faces, necks, and tails.

- Length: 9 to 11 inches

Quaker parakeets like to spend time out of their cages and might even learn to let themselves out!

Chapter 10

Quaker Parakeet

These large parakeets are from such South American countries as Argentina, Brazil, and Uruguay. Quaker parakeets are also called monk parakeets.

General Behavior

Quaker parakeets:

1. are talkative and lively.

2. can learn tricks.

3. are able to escape their cage sometimes.

4. can be very noisy.

5. live 25 to 30 years.

Special Needs

Like other large parakeets, Quaker parakeets need a large cage that is at least 24 inches long by 24 inches wide by 36 inches high. They need a lot of exercise, so make sure to let them out of the cage often to play.

Keeping Your Bird Healthy

The best way to keep your pet bird healthy is to protect it from danger. You may not see it, but there is danger all around your home. Some things that are harmless to humans can really hurt your bird.

Remove poisonous plants, such as English ivy and mistletoe, from your home. These plants are poisonous to other animals and humans, too. To find

Keeping Your Bird Healthy

out what plants are dangerous, visit animal and human poison control Web sites or read books on poisonous plants.

Do not let your bird go into the bathroom or kitchen. It could get hurt by flying into a toilet or an uncovered pot cooking on the stove.

Close the curtains or shades before you let the bird out of its cage. The bird cannot see the glass and can injure itself by trying to fly out of a closed window.

Beware of things in your home that give off fumes. Birds are more sensitive to certain chemicals than humans. Fumes from household cleaners, candles, Teflon-coated cookware, and many other items can be poisonous to your bird.

It is also important to make sure your bird has good care every day. Provide fresh food and water. Keep your eyes on your bird if you take it out of its cage for exercise. If your bird will not go back into its cage, try putting a healthy treat in the cage. This might make your bird want to go back in!

A clean cage will help keep your bird healthy. Be sure to clean its toys, too!

Keeping Your Bird Healthy

Ask your vet about special grooming needs. Some birds need their beaks and nails trimmed. Others need to be misted with water.

Keeping things clean will also help your bird stay well. Change the cage paper often and wash food and water dishes daily. Once a week, give the cage a good scrub.

Simply watching your bird is another way to care for its health. If your bird starts eating or drinking less, it may be sick. Any big change in how your bird acts may be its way of telling you that it is ill. Loud or heavy breathing, throwing up, or blood in its droppings are other signs that a bird may be sick.

If you think that your bird is sick, tell the vet about the signs of illness you noticed in your bird. Give the vet some information about the bird's age, past illnesses, and its diet.

While birds can be a lot of work, they also can be great pets and companions. By giving your bird the best care, you can help your pet stay healthy and create a longtime friend.

Glossary

avian veterinarian (vet)—An animal doctor who takes care of birds.

breeder—A person who raises birds that are bred to look and act a certain way.

crest—A group of feathers that sticks up from a bird's head.

hand-fed—A way of raising birds by taking them from their parents to be cared for by humans.

pellets—A type of bird food.

perch—A rod for a bird to rest on.

rescue group—An organization that rescues unwanted animals and finds homes for them.

species—A specific type of animal. Animals of the same species can produce young together.

tamed—Not wild. Raised to live with and depend on humans.

vent—A small area on the underside of a bird that it can open to release its waste.

Further Reading

Blackaby, Susan. *A Bird for You: Caring for Your Bird.* Mankato, Minn.: Picture Window Books, 2003.

Gillis, Jennifer Bilzin. *Birds.* Chicago: Heinemann Library, 2004.

Jeffrey, Laura S. *Birds: How to Choose and Care for a Bird.* Berkeley Heights, N.J.: Enslow, 2004.

Waters, Jo. *The Wild Side of Pet Birds.* Chicago: Raintree, 2005.

Index